Your Inner Child

YOUR INNER CHILD

**A Guided Journal
to Heal Your Past and
Recover Your Joy**

Kelly Bramblett

ROCKRIDGE
PRESS

Copyright © 2022 by Rockridge Press

First Rockridge Press trade paperback edition 2022

Rockridge Press and the Rockridge Press logo are trademarks or registered trademarks of Callisto Media Inc. and/or its affiliates in the United States and other countries and may not be used without written permission.

For general information on our other products and services, please contact our Customer Care Department within the United States at (866) 744-2665, or outside the United States at (510) 253-0500.

Paperback ISBN: 978-1-68539-274-1

Manufactured in the United States of America

Interior and Cover Designer: Erik Jacobsen
Art Producer: Melissa Malinowsky
Editor: Adrian Potts
Production Editor: Dylan Julian
Production Manager: Lanore Coloprisco

Illustrations © iStock, cover and pp. ii, v, vi, xii, 6, 10, 14, 26, 35, 41, 48, 52, 54, 63, 76, 78, 93, 100, 102, 108, 112, 118, 125
All other illustrations used under license from Shutterstock.com

10 9 8 7 6 5 4 3 2 1 0

This journal belongs to:

....

Contents

Introduction ix

How to Use This Book xi

Section 1: Embracing Your Inner Child 1

Section 2: Understanding Your Inner Child's Wounds 27

Section 3: Exploring the Legacy of Your Childhood 55

Section 4: Meeting Your Inner Child's Needs 79

Section 5: Nurturing Your Inner Child Every Day 103

A Final Note 126

Resources 127

References 129

Introduction

First and foremost, I want to welcome you to the beginning of a new and exciting inner journey. I congratulate you for taking this step toward your own personal development and healing goals.

Before we get started, I would like to share a bit about myself and what has led me to this work. My name is Kelly Bramblett, and I am a trauma care specialist, a general life coach, and a law of attraction practitioner. Having suffered sexual, emotional, and physical abuse that started in early childhood and continued through adulthood, I have learned firsthand how beneficial practices like inner child work can be for healing unresolved trauma. This understanding through my own experience has fueled my passion for guiding others through this work as well.

If you are new to this topic, you may be wondering what inner child work is and what it entails. Inner child work is a trauma-informed approach to helping people who have experienced childhood trauma confront and heal their wounding at the originating source. Trauma itself comes in many forms. It can be the result of abuse and neglect, and it can show up in subtle ways that can be difficult to identify and can stem from anything that created a strong, negative emotional reaction that left a lasting impression.

Your inner child is the childlike aspect within your psyche and includes any conditioned thinking learned or formed before puberty. Through your work in this book, you will discover how to reparent your inner child so that your past painful experiences no longer negatively impact your present-day self.

Journaling is one of my favorite tools when doing inner work and has been a practice I have relied on since I was a young girl. Often when we are writing, we aren't overthinking our words, and it allows those hidden, subconscious narratives to surface. Awareness is the key piece to all personal development; without it, no growth can happen.

While this journal is an excellent tool to help guide you through inner child work, it does not replace the advice of a therapist or other trained professional. If you feel overwhelmed with feelings of anxiety or depression, I encourage you to find additional support. There is no shame in advocating for yourself and reaching out for help if it's needed.

The idea of facing your past painful experiences may sound daunting or even frightening, but it is my intention to help you connect to your inner child through fun and enjoyment in the exercises and practices I will share with you. That doesn't mean you won't experience some difficult emotions as you heal your inner child, but it will be well worth the effort and commitment. Growth happens in small, subtle, but sustainable steps. Often, we don't realize how far we have come until, one day, we realize that we are less triggered and more satisfied in our lives. It is my deepest honor to guide you through this work. Thank you for trusting me to be a part of your story.

All my love,
Kelly

How to Use This Book

This journal is divided into five sections based on different inner child work topics. You will find journal prompts, affirmations, and exercises to help guide you in each section. In addition to those elements, there are suggested practices that you can do outside this book to help you embody the lessons presented to you.

The journal sections are sequenced in a way that reflects the natural progression of inner child work in a therapeutic setting. However, everybody's journey is unique, and how you choose to work through your journal is entirely up to you. You might feel like you want to start at the beginning and work through in order, beginning to end. Or you may choose to work through the lessons that most resonate with you at the time. Do what feels right. There is no right or wrong way to navigate through this journal, so have fun with it and trust your intuition.

There is also no time frame for you to complete the material in this book. In fact, taking short breaks can help bring more potency to the practices, as doing so allows time for the information to settle into the subconscious mind. Don't push yourself; remember, there is no final destination when it comes to healing and personal growth. Move at a pace that feels good for you. Again, if you feel triggered to the point that it feels unmanageable, take a break and seek additional support.

SECTION 1

Embracing Your Inner Child

Just like with any other new relationship in your life, you need to take time to get to understand the aspect of yourself that makes up your inner child. Expect that they may be shy or quiet initially. This will be especially true if this part of you has been repressed or ignored for a long time. Approach your inner child with unconditional love and compassion to strengthen the bond. It can take time to build trust with your inner child, but remaining patient with yourself through the process will facilitate this. Stick to doing the work, and you will begin to quickly recognize that little voice within and identify their needs.

In the first section of this book, you will discover your inner child by focusing on elements of your childhood. I will guide you in creating a solid relationship with this aspect of yourself that will serve as the foundation you will build upon as you continue your inner child journey. As previously mentioned, I will do this by offering you journal prompts, affirmations, exercises, and practices designed to support you and your inner child.

How would you describe your early years? What emotions show up when you think back to your childhood experiences?

What words of comfort, support, or guidance do you wish you would have received as a child? Who did you most need to hear these things from and why?

What do you think it would have felt like to hear the affirming and supportive messages you needed as a child? How might it have changed how you saw the world?

Breathwork to Center and Calm You

One of the most powerful tools at your disposal is your breath. By focusing on your breath, you can soothe your nervous system and return to a calmer, more centered you. While this breathwork practice begins the journal, I encourage you to return to it each time you work with this book. Doing so will create a comfortable space within your body as you are confronted by content that may be triggering.

One of the most significant benefits of self-regulation practices like box breathing, which you will learn here, is that it causes your fight-or-flight response to shut down and activates the frontal lobes in the brain. The frontal lobes are responsible for decision-making, logic, planning, and clear thinking. Techniques like this one will help you shift from reactiveness to responsiveness.

Before you begin, on a scale of 1 to 10—with 1 being completely relaxed and 10 being anxious and out of sorts—rate how you feel before practicing box breathing. _____

1. Find a comfortable space where you can sit or lie down if that feels nice. Make sure that you will be uninterrupted so you can fully focus on yourself.

2. Focus on your breath while gradually deepening it with each inhalation. As you exhale, visualize any stress, worry, and responsibilities you may be focused on leaving your body through the breath. You may choose to place your hands over your heart to create an even deeper connection to your physical body.

3. Notice where you are tensing muscles in your body and consciously release those muscles, bringing the body and mind into a relaxed state.

4. Begin box breathing by inhaling for a count of five, holding the lungs full for a count of three, releasing the breath through the nose for a count of five, and then holding the lungs empty for three. This is considered one full cycle.

5. Feel free to play with the length of time you are holding and releasing, gradually working your way to five counts for all phases of the breathwork.

6. Continue the practice for three minutes if you are new to mindfulness and meditative practices. If you are more experienced, you may want to start at five, ten, or fifteen minutes. You can set a timer on your phone to alert you when the time is up.

Once you have finished, rate how you feel on the same ten-point scale I mentioned earlier. _____

What were some of your favorite games, toys, or activities as a child? Go into detail about why these activities brought you so much joy. If you didn't have a childhood that involved fun, write about what you always wanted or wished you could do. It's okay if these questions make you sad for your younger self. Grieving is a healthy emotion, and it is safe for you to feel your feelings.

It is safe for me to come into my body while doing this work.

How Does Your Inner Child Like to Play?

The following checklist will help bring clarity to how your inner child likes to play. There are two options for completing the exercise. You can check the items you may have enjoyed as a child but have long stopped doing, or you can check the items your younger self didn't get to participate in but would have liked to (or would still like to). Space is provided at the end to write down any activities not included on the list.

☐ Coloring

☐ Going to the park

☐ Dancing or singing

☐ Blowing bubbles

☐ Spending time playing outside

☐ Playing with friends

☐ Participating in sports

☐ Playing board games

☐ Building things

☐ Reading

☐ Watching movies

☐ Trading cards

☐ Playing video games

☐ Collecting things

☐ Playing make-believe

☐ Painting or crafting

☐ Playing dress-up

☐ Playing with your favorite toys

☐ Participating in group activities or clubs

☐ Going to the zoo, beaches, amusement parks, camping trips, and so on

☐ ....

☐ ....

☐ ....

☐ ....

Connecting with Your Inner Child through Play

U se the checklist on the previous page to explore new ways to connect with your inner child by doing some of those activities in the coming days and weeks. You can start with your childhood favorites, or you may choose to start with things you didn't have a chance to experience as a child. Try to work your way through the entire list by picking one new thing to try each week.

If you feel silly, think about how children behave. They are never worried about how others perceive them; they are free, joyful, and unconcerned with appearances. Try to connect to that same energy you felt as a child, and most important, have fun!

Think back to a time in childhood when you were playful. What emotions did you feel, and how can you bring more of those feel-good emotions into your life as an adult?

Write about the things, people, and experiences that bring you joy as an adult. These may be things you already do or that you wish to do more of. As you are writing, contemplate how often you allow yourself to feel joyfulness and explore any thoughts that show up around this topic.

*I allow myself to
experience joyfulness
for the sake of simply
being joyful.*

Connecting with Your Younger Self

For this practice, you will need one or more photographs of you as a child. If you have several showing you at different ages, you can use multiple, but one will work just as well. These should be photographs of you before the age of puberty. The exception to this may be if you experienced some major trauma in your later youth and you wish to connect with your inner child at that age to help heal that specific trauma. Next, you will:

1. Choose a private space in your home to display your photograph(s). It should be a place you feel comfortable spending time in.

2. Visit your photo each day and examine it.

3. Try to remember what was happening in your life at that time. For example, how did you feel? What things were going well, and what things weren't? How did you spend your days?

4. Use the following page to journal anything that seems important or relevant after each session.

What are you learning about your childhood as you spend time each day with your photograph(s)? What thoughts, feelings, and memories arise? What aspects of this practice surprise you?

Who made a significant impression in your life as a child? How did they do so, and were the experiences positive or negative ones? How have those experiences impacted how you think or act as an adult?

It is okay for me to feel sadness or grief for the joyful parts of childhood I missed out on.

Starting a Dialogue with Your Inner Child

As you spend time connecting to your past self, you may choose to begin a dialogue with your inner child. The best way to do this is to ask your inner child questions and then write down the first thing that comes to mind. Don't overthink your answers, as this may block the process. There is no right or wrong way to go about this; it's simply a tool for you to explore. You can ask these questions while looking at old pictures of yourself or just visualizing your younger self.

1. What do you need more of?

2. What are your fears and insecurities?

3. What do you need to feel safe?

4. What things do you feel are your fault, and why?

....

....

....

5. Who makes you feel the best, most loved, or safest?

....

....

....

6. What situations make you feel scared, uneasy, or unsafe, and why?

....

....

....

7. Where do you feel the most comfortable?

....

....

....

8. What makes you feel sad, and why?

9. What makes you feel happy, and why?

10. Where is your favorite place to spend time, and why?

How Does Your Inner Child React?

When children become stressed, tired, or overstimulated, they tend to react to their emotions instantly and without thinking. This reactivity can live on through our inner child. Answer the following questions by circling the response that best describes how you react to challenging situations. This helps you gain awareness of any patterns so that you can continue exploring them throughout this journal.

When faced with painful experiences, I tend to:

Shut down   Go into action

Cry   Scream

Internalize   Vocalize

Look for the lessons   Wonder "Why me?"

When I am embarrassed, I tend to:

Obsess   Avoid

Hide   Project

Deny   Take accountability

Laugh at myself   Self-loathe

When I am angry, I tend to:

Name call   Run away

Shut down   Lash out

React in the moment   Pause, and choose how
                                  I wish to respond
Lose control
                                  Stay grounded

What did you learn about the way you react to strong emotions from the last exercise? What areas are you the strongest in, and what areas do you need to work on? Were you surprised by any of your answers? If so, why?

How comfortable are you sitting with your heavy emotions? What do you fear about allowing yourself the space to feel whatever shows up? Can you express your emotions to others in a productive manner?

Use this space to write a letter from your younger self to your adult self now. It may help to imagine yourself at a specific age, such as 5 or 10 years old. What would they want you to know? What feelings would they express? What comfort, encouragement, or admiration would they offer to you now?

Continued >>

Continued >>

Understanding Your Inner Child's Wounds

C hildhood wounds can take many forms. Almost all of us have past painful experiences from our early years that still impact our lives as adults. For some, there may have been a clear pattern of abuse or neglect. If that was true for you, inner child work can be of great benefit. I would also recommend reaching out to a therapist or other trained professional for more support if you haven't already (see the Resources on page 127).

For others, childhood trauma can take more subtle forms, sometimes arising from mistakes our parents made. Most of our parents weren't blessed with the tools, support, and resources we have today, and the further back we go in our lineage, the more this rings true; our grandparents had even less support than our parents, and our great-grandparents had yet even less than them, and so on.

It is common for adults to accept dysfunction presented in our childhood or families as normal, healthy, or even beneficial. In this section, I will guide you to awareness by helping you identify your inherited conditioned thinking and childhood wounding.

Identifying Childhood Trauma

As I mentioned in the introduction of this section, our minds will often automatically go to thoughts of abuse and neglect when we hear the term *childhood trauma*. However, childhood trauma encompasses many other things. This exercise will help bring awareness to painful childhood experiences that you might not associate with trauma. Put a check mark next to anything from the following list that applies to your childhood experience.

☐ Emotional immaturity or mood swings from your parents or caregivers

☐ A parental figure who ignored you, wasn't invested in your life, or didn't spend time with you

☐ Not feeling safe or protected by your parental figures

☐ Not having your emotions validated or your emotional needs met as a child

☐ Not having your basic needs met (e.g., clothes, shelter, or food)

☐ Parents who often fought in front of you

☐ A parental figure who battled addiction

☐ A parent who inappropriately shared their problems or depended on you for their emotional security, causing you, as a child, to have to step into the parenting role

☐ A parent or caregiver with a mental illness such as a personality disorder, depression, or anxiety (particularly if untreated)

☐ Loss of a parent as a child to death, abandonment, or other circumstances

☐ Bullying by family members or schoolmates

☐ Community violence

☐ A life-threatening illness or having a serious accident

What were some of the things you identified in the previous exercise that surprised you, and why?

_____

_____

_____

_____

_____

_____

_____

_____

_____

_____

_____

_____

_____

How did those things you marked make you feel as a child, and in which ways did they impact your overall experience?

_____

_____

_____

_____

_____

_____

_____

_____

_____

_____

_____

_____

I can easily validate my own experiences, even if someone disagrees with my perception of them.

Connecting with Your Memories

Connecting with your earliest childhood memories is a powerful way to create a deep connection with your inner child because it takes you back to what you thought, felt, and experienced in those moments. If your childhood had an element of trauma, you might not have many memories, but don't let that deter you from this exercise. Whether you have vivid memories or seemingly none, as you connect with what you do recall, the more that will come to the surface.

Be patient with this process. This exercise works best if you let go of any expectations and accept what unfolds. If the memories surfacing cause distress, panic, or are just too uncomfortable, pause and recenter yourself by taking deep breaths and relaxing the body.

When you are ready, close your eyes and think about one of your earliest childhood memories. Spend some time observing all that you can recall before answering the following questions. Remember, it doesn't matter if you are two years old in your memory or fifteen. Just observe what shows up.

What are you doing in this memory?

....

....

What stands out to you about this memory?

....

....

How are you feeling in your memory?

....

....

What sights or sounds can you pinpoint?

....

....

Are there other people around, and what are they doing?

....

....

What other details seem important?

....

....

Meet Your Inner Child Meditation

This is a simple practice to further connect with your inner child. You can use this time spent with your inner child in meditation to ask questions or offer support and love to them.

1. Find a comfortable space where you won't be disturbed. You may even choose some relaxing music to set the mood for this meditation practice.

2. Begin focusing on your breath while seated or lying down to relax, deepening the inhalation and releasing any tension in your body with the exhalation.

3. Once you feel relaxed, visualize yourself standing outside in a forest on a path that leads you through the woods. Take time to allow the details of this image to form. You may see forest creatures or hear the birds chirping. You may notice wildflowers or green grassy patches alongside your path. Is your path dirt, or is it paved?

4. Start traveling the path, walking until you notice a clearing that opens to a beautiful meadow filled with flowers and butterflies.

5. Notice a single oak tree in the distance. As you approach the tree, you see a small figure sitting alone under it, and you feel instantly drawn to them.

6. Recognize the small figure coming into focus as your younger self. Take note here of how they appear. For example, are they happy, or do they seem upset or look scared?

7. Sit down next to your younger self under the tree. Take time to converse with them. You may ask how they feel, what they are scared of, or what they need to feel safe. These are just examples to get you started. Use your intuition when asking your own questions.

8. Say goodbye to your younger self when you feel satisfied with the time spent here, and come back into the room you are in by wiggling your hands and toes and allowing your eyes to softly open.

What messages did your inner child share with you in the meditation?

What emotions showed up for you during the time spent with your younger self, and what insight do you have on those emotions?

_____

_____

_____

_____

_____

_____

_____

_____

_____

_____

_____

_____

_____

I listen to my inner child's needs with love and acceptance.

What emotional needs did you have as a child that weren't met? For example, did you need more time, more affection, more patience, or more love from your parent or caregiver?

How did not having those needs met as a child make you feel? What thoughts surface today when you ponder this issue?

_____

_____

_____

_____

_____

_____

_____

_____

_____

_____

_____

_____

Mirror Work to Reparent Your Inner Child

Now that you have identified some of your inner child's unmet needs, you can use this practice to reparent yourself. *Reparenting* refers to giving yourself what you didn't receive as a child. Stand in the mirror, gazing into your eyes, and sense the presence of your inner child coming forth. Start speaking loving messages to them. For example, if your need to feel safe wasn't met as a child, you may say, "You are safe," "I am here," and "I will always protect you." Or if your need for praise and approval wasn't met, you may say things like "You are doing so well," "I am so proud of you," and "I love you so much." This practice can be uncomfortable at first, but that is what makes it so powerful. Pushing past our comfort zone is how we grow.

Reflection on Mirror Work

Use this space to write about your experience with the reparenting mirror practice. What phrases did you use during this exercise, and why?

How did your inner child respond to your praise?

Did your inner child share anything with you during the practice, and if so, what?

What emotions did you feel during this exercise?

_____

_____

_____

What other observations did you make during the mirror
work exercise?

_____

_____

_____

_____

_____

_____

_____

_____

_____

_____

I honor my inner child's needs to be seen and heard by listening with intent.

What is an experience that may seem insignificant to others but deeply upset or embarrassed you as a child? What words of reassurance would you offer to your younger self about the experience?

Adverse Childhood Experiences (ACEs)

An adverse childhood experience (ACE) score is a tally of different types of abuse, neglect, and unsettling childhood experiences. The higher the score, the greater the risk of mental and physical health problems in adulthood, according to the adverse childhood experience study conducted by the Centers for Disease Control and Prevention and Kaiser Permanente. This exercise will help you gain additional awareness of your past traumatic experiences and how they may be affecting your life today. ACEs was developed by Dr. Robert Anda, Dr. Vincent Felitti, and their associates.

Trigger warning: Some of the material covered in the test may stir up uncomfortable memories. If you feel overwhelmed at any point, take a break and come back to this exercise when you feel ready.

For each "yes" answer, add a tally mark in the space at the end of the questionnaire on page 48. The total number of tally marks is your cumulative number of ACEs.

1. Did a parent or other adult in the household often or very often:

   a. Swear at you, insult you, put you down, or humiliate you?

   b. Act in a way that made you afraid that you might be physically hurt?

2. Did a parent or other adult in the household often or very often:

   a. Push, grab, slap, or throw something at you?

   b. Hit you so hard that you had marks or were injured?

3. Did an adult or person at least five years older than you ever:

   a. Touch or fondle you or have you touch their body in a sexual way?

   b. Attempt to or actually have oral, anal, or vaginal intercourse with you?

4. Did you often or very often feel that:

   a. No one in your family loved you or thought you were important or special?

   b. Your family didn't look out for each other, feel close to each other, or support each other?

5. Did you often or very often feel that:

   a. You didn't have enough to eat, had to wear dirty clothes, and had no one to protect you?

   b. Your parents were too drunk or high to take care of you or take you to the doctor if you needed it?

6. Were your parents ever separated or divorced?

7. Was your mother, stepmother, or guardian:

   a. Often or very often pushed, grabbed, slapped, or had something thrown at her?

   b. Sometimes, often, or very often kicked, bitten, hit with a fist, or hit with something hard?

   c. Ever repeatedly hit over at least a few minutes or threatened with a gun or knife?

Continued >>

Continued >>

8. Did you live with anyone who was a problem drinker or alcoholic or who used street drugs?

9. Was a household member depressed or mentally ill, or did a household member attempt suicide?

10. Did a household member go to prison?

Total tally marks: ....

High ACE scores have been linked to a wide range of mental and physical health problems in adulthood, including heart disease and general anxiety disorder. What was your ACE score, and were you surprised by it? Did taking this test change your perception of your childhood? If so, how?

How do you feel your childhood experience has affected you as an adult?

What emotions showed up as you completed the questionnaire? Do you feel able to be with these heavy emotions to process them? If you feel overwhelmed, remember that you can move on to another page and return to this section when you feel able to. A practice like The Thirty-Second Hug (page 108) or Breathwork to Center and Calm You (page 5) may be helpful to ground yourself.

Heal Your Inner Child through Silliness and Movement

Because there has been a fair amount of heaviness in this section, let's end it on a lighter note. Movement will help you release old energy that may have been stirred up from some of the previous practices and exercises. Silliness will lighten your mood and help you connect with joy.

For this practice, put on some of your cheesiest dance tunes and move your body! Don't overthink your movements; it's not a dance contest, and no one is watching. You may get down on the floor, jump around, make silly faces, scream with delight, sing at the top of your lungs, or twirl around until you are dizzy. Embody the movements and attitude of a child. Have fun with this.

SECTION 3

Exploring the Legacy of Your Childhood

We often aren't fully aware of how our childhood wounding affects our current reality. We must illuminate the subconscious mind to discover the originating source of unhealthy patterns and cycles in which we are currently participating. An example of what this looks like showed up in my life recently as I was connecting the dots between the consistent feeling of not being safe as a child and my often-irrational fears as an adult. I was able to see that my need for structure to feel safe today results from my attempts to control situations as a child to create a feeling of security that was lacking for me at the time.

The great news is that once we connect these dots and can clearly see how our past painful experiences from childhood have shaped our current patterns, we can write a new story. The prompts, exercises, and practices in this section will bring more awareness to how your past painful childhood experiences affect your life today.

Connecting the Dots

It's time to connect the dots between past painful experiences and your current patterns.

1. Identify a childhood trauma event or experience.
    Example: *My father was a heavy drinker and often became aggressive or hostile.*

----

2. How did it impact you at the time?
    Example: *I often felt unsafe when he would drink, even when he didn't become aggressive; just the possibility of it would scare me.*

----

3. How did the experience shape the way you view things today?
Example: I associate drinking with danger and feel uncomfortable when people around me are overindulging.

_____

_____

_____

_____

_____

4. To what cycle or pattern is this experience connected today?
Example: I will often try to control situations to avoid feeling anxious or uncomfortable and am seen as being a control freak by others.

_____

_____

_____

_____

_____

_____

With awareness, I can easily break cycles that no longer serve me.

Describe in detail a place where you felt the safest as a child, and explain why.

Who is someone you looked up to or deeply respected as a child? What values, qualities, and actions of theirs did you admire?

Can you remember the first time an important person in your life disappointed you? Describe the experience here.

....

....

....

....

....

How do you feel now when people disappoint you in your life? Note any similarities in how you felt as a child and how you feel now in the face of disappointment.

....

....

....

....

....

How would you summarize your childhood experience? What key themes or patterns can you identify in how you view your childhood experiences?

In what ways have these themes or patterns carried forward into your adult life?

Breaking Cycles

Now that you are aware of how painful experiences from childhood affect your life today, it's time to begin breaking long-held patterns that are negatively impacting your life. This process requires you to begin thinking and responding in a new way, which takes consistency and work. The good news is that it only takes twenty-one days to create a new habit, which means it will get easier with each day.

For the next twenty-one days, when you observe yourself thinking or engaging in your usual tendencies, stop and immediately choose something different that is more serving. For example, if you have often sought outside validation from others, you may instead choose to practice more self-love and self-acceptance. You can do this by spending extra time on self-care.

For this practice to be successful, you must be a nonjudgmental observer, which means being gentle and loving toward yourself as your awareness grows.

Tracking Your Progress

Return to these questions once you have practiced creating new habits for at least twenty-one days. Mark it on your calendar or set an alert on your phone to help you remember.

1. What habits or tendencies did you work on changing over the past three weeks?

....

....

....

2. When did you notice the habits or tendencies emerging (e.g., in certain situations or places)?

....

....

....

3. What did you choose to do differently that was more helpful to you when you became aware of the tendencies or habits?

....

....

....

4. In what ways and areas did your life improve through the practice of intentionality and choosing something different than you have always done before?

_____

_____

_____

5. What did you learn about yourself during the twenty-one days of self-awareness and observation?

_____

_____

_____

_____

_____

_____

_____

_____

_____

Writing a New Story

It is often the stories birthed from our childhood experiences that keep us stuck in our toxic cycles and patterns. Writing a new narrative can move us to a healthier space and ultimately reshape our current experience. This exercise has two parts. First, you must identify your old stories, and then you must create something new. For example, a person who grew up with a mother who often criticized them and placed unrealistic expectations on them may have grown into an adult with people-pleasing tendencies. Because of this, they created a story that says that to be worthy of love and acceptance, they must please others. A new, more helpful story might be that they are worthy of love, affection, validation, and appreciation with no strings attached. Use this exercise to guide you through rewriting one of your own stories.

Identify a long-held narrative and use the space to write about it.

I have the power to create my own story and shape my experiences in a way that facilitates peace and joy.

Now that you have clarity on your old narrative, it's time to rewrite your story. What is a narrative that feels more helpful to you?

Continued >>

Continued >>

....

....

....

....

....

....

....

....

....

....

....

....

Revisit your new story each morning by reading it aloud. Doing this will reinforce this new narrative so that it becomes the prominent story you tell.

I release guilt over things that are not mine to feel remorse over.

Healing Shame around Childhood Experiences

There is a subtle difference between guilt and shame. Guilt is a helpful emotion that lets us know when we have acted outside our core values and allows us to pivot and realign. Shame develops when we either can't forgive ourselves for our behavior or continue the behavior instead of realigning. It is common for children to experience guilt over things that, in reality, have nothing to do with them, such as their parents' divorce or abuse that occurred. As the children grow, the guilt can develop into deep-seated shame. This stored shame can manifest in many unhealthy ways, such as feelings of unworthiness or self-sabotaging behavior. Use the space to write about an experience in your childhood that has created shame. As you are writing, consider how you can bring compassion to your younger self.

How has holding on to guilt and shame for things that weren't yours to carry caused you to think and feel about yourself as an adult?

How would your thinking about yourself change if you gave yourself permission to release the shameful emotions you hold around painful experiences from your childhood?

Fire Ritual for Releasing Stored Shame

The following activity is designed to help you release shame. Work with fire in a designated safe space only, such as a fireplace or outdoor firepit.

1. Find a blank piece of paper (outside this journal) and write down all the ways you have been impacted by holding on to shame over a past experience. For example, it could be that you feel anger, sadness, or self-loathing or that you have been afraid to be vulnerable with others.

2. Burn your paper in the fire and imagine your long-held shame being carried away with the smoke.

3. Take a deep breath when you are finished and release the breath through your mouth audibly for an even deeper release.

Meeting Your Inner Child's Needs

As is often said, parenting doesn't come with a training manual. Most parents get thrown into the job only with what they have been taught or what they have managed to learn by the time they decide to have children. This reality leads to many mistakes, as individuals navigate their way through parenting while contending with their own experiences, needs, wounding, conditioned thinking, and mindset. Those of you who are parents know firsthand how difficult it can be to know what the right thing is for each child and in each situation.

Most parents can only do the best they can with the resources, tools, and knowledge they possess. This is why everyone experiences childhood trauma, has needs go unmet, or is exposed to dysfunction. It doesn't mean we have "bad" parents; it just means they are human and made mistakes while learning and growing with us.

A big part of inner child work is examining where our parents or other caregivers may have fallen short in meeting our needs and then meeting those needs for ourselves. This section will be focused on guiding you through reparenting so that you can find peace and acceptance for your past, regardless of the difficulties you experienced.

A boundary is a guideline you have that lets people know how you want to be treated and what you're willing to accept or not accept. What were you taught about boundaries growing up? How has this impacted how you create and hold boundaries today?

Where do you feel you struggle most to hold your boundaries, and why do you think this is? How does this relate to your child-hood experiences around these boundaries?

Exploring Your Boundaries

We first learn boundaries in childhood, but if we have been taught or shown weak boundaries growing up, we tend to hold weak boundaries as adults. In this exercise, you will explore three categories to clarify your limits. Following are some questions to help you clarify your boundaries.

PERSONAL BOUNDARIES

Personal boundaries refer to your body and personal space. Take some time to consider what yours are using the following questions to guide your reflection.

- How much alone time do you need to feel grounded and happy?

- How do you feel comfortable being touched (e.g., hugs, handshakes, etc.) by other people?

- Are there people in your life who invade your personal space in a way you are not comfortable with?

- What are your personal spaces, and who is allowed in them (e.g., Is your bedroom off-limits to your children? Is your art space off-limits to everyone? Is your office a no-go zone for family?)?

- How much physical space do you need in public settings to feel comfortable?

Write down what your personal boundaries are and/or what you would like them to be.

_____

_____

_____

_____

_____

_____

EMOTIONAL BOUNDARIES

Now let's explore what your emotional boundaries are. These relate to what you feel comfortable sharing and receiving emotionally from others. Here are some questions to guide your reflection.

- Whom do you feel comfortable being vulnerable with in your life, and whom do you not?

- Are there people in your life who share things that make you uncomfortable or leave you feeling drained?

- Is there a balance between give and take in sharing and space-holding with the people in your life (e.g., Are you able to express your emotions and also allow others to do the same, or do you allow people to emotionally dump on you or vice versa?)?

- Do you feel like your voice matters? Are there people in your life who you wish heard you more clearly when you express your needs?

- Are you able to express your emotional needs to those in your life? What are those needs?

- What do you need emotionally from a partner to feel safe and comfortable in the relationship?

Write down what your emotional boundaries are and/or what you would like them to be.

SEXUAL BOUNDARIES

Finally, let's explore what your sexual boundaries are. These determine what is okay and what isn't for you sexually.

1. How comfortable are you saying no to things during sexual encounters that make you uncomfortable?

2. What are your limits in the bedroom?

3. What do you need sexually from a partner to feel satisfied?

4. Do you feel it's okay to have sex when you don't feel like it to satisfy a partner's needs, or is this something that is not okay?

5. Is being emotionally connected to your sexual partner important to you?

Write down what your sexual boundaries are and/or what you would like them to be.

....

....

....

....

....

....

Putting Your Boundaries into Practice

The exercise on the previous pages should have helped you clarify your boundaries, but now it is time to put them into practice. If you have held weak boundaries up to this point, as you begin to more strongly enforce them, people in your life will likely resist and not take kindly to the changes you are making. The important people in your life will adjust, but change is always scary and your loved ones may react negatively to changes you are making for yourself that directly impact them. Some people may fall away; it's okay to let them go. Remember, you are making space for healthier energies and relationships.

Use the space provided to brainstorm how you can communicate, set, and maintain your boundaries with family, your partner, your colleagues, strangers, or anyone else. It's okay to start small, such as by asking a friend who always shows up unannounced to call before just stopping by to visit.

How I will communicate, set, and maintain my personal boundaries:

How I will communicate, set, and maintain my emotional boundaries:

....

....

....

....

....

How I will communicate, set, and maintain my sexual boundaries:

....

....

....

....

....

It is safe for me to create and hold healthy boundaries even if it upsets some people.

What Needs Were Unmet?

This is an exercise to help you clarify what unmet needs you may have had as a child so that you can then start meeting them. In the list, you will find common essential conditions children require to feel healthy and happy. Check any you did not have met as a child (or that were only met some of the time). Space is provided to write down any other needs you may not have had met.

☐ Security

☐ Love

☐ Structure

☐ Routine

☐ Patience

☐ Affection

☐ Positive praise

☐ Basic needs for survival (i.e., clean clothes, food, and shelter)

☐ Stability

☐ Medical/dental care

☐ Protection

☐ Consistency

☐ Socialization with peers

☐ Other: _____

☐ Other: _____

☐ Other: _____

☐ Other: _____

How do you think your neglected needs as a child have affected you as an adult?

_____

_____

_____

_____

_____

_____

_____

_____

_____

_____

_____

_____

_____

Meeting Your Inner Child's Needs

On the left side of the page, list your unmet needs as a child, referencing the checklist on page 89. On the right side, brainstorm ways to meet these needs as an adult.

CHILDHOOD UNMET NEED	HOW I CAN HONOR THIS NEED NOW

I am able to meet my needs with ease.

Butterfly Hug to Soothe Your Inner Child

The Butterfly Hug is a tapping practice that is great to have in your toolbox for when your inner child is feeling scared. First developed by Lucina Artigas, it can be used anytime you want to regulate the nervous system quickly. This practice is so soothing because the tapping mimics the mother's heartbeat in the womb and signals to the brain that it is safe to relax.

1. Cross your hands over your chest with your palms facing the body. Place the hands so that the top of each middle finger rests below the opposite collarbone.

2. Interlock your thumbs, making a butterfly shape with the hands.

3. Slowly tap your hands on your chest, alternating between your left and right hand, in a rhythmic beat.

4. As you tap, breathe in and exhale deeply.

5. Continue tapping for as long as it feels good or until you feel relief.

Extending Forgiveness

Almost everyone suffers during childhood due to the actions of others. Extending forgiveness to those people sets you free from carrying the burden of the traumatic experience. Respond to the following prompts. You will use this information for the next practice.

Recall a person or group of people who created a painful experience for you during childhood. Write about the incident briefly.

Write down the name(s) of the person or people who caused your wounding.

Work through each person listed on the previous page and decide, on a scale of 1 to 10—with 1 being no resistance and 10 being complete resistance—how comfortable you are extending forgiveness to each individual.

Metta Meditation for Forgiveness

Metta meditation is a Buddhist practice also sometimes referred to as loving-kindness meditation. While it can be used to send well wishes to anyone, it is an incredibly potent practice when used with a person who requires our forgiveness. To forgive those who have harmed us doesn't mean we are letting them off the hook or that we have to allow them to be a part of our life. Extending forgiveness is a gift you give to yourself that ends your suffering and allows your inner child to heal. Work through the names you listed in the previous exercise for this practice. Choose the person you have the least resistance to forgiving first, and gradually work your way to those you have the most resistance to forgiving.

1. Find a comfortable position and let yourself picture the person you wish to forgive.

2. Reflect on how they hurt you as a child and allow yourself to feel the sorrow you have carried from the past.

3. Let yourself know that you can release the burden of this pain by extending forgiveness when your heart is ready. Say out loud: "I have carried this pain for too long. To the extent that I am ready, I offer forgiveness."

4. Extend loving-kindness to the person with the following mantras:

   - "May [person's name] have peace."

   - "May [person's name] have love."

   - "May [person's name] have healing."

   - "May [person's name] feel supported."

Forgiving those who harmed me doesn't mean what they did was okay; it only means I am no longer willing to suffer.

How does your inner child react when you extend forgiveness to those who harmed them, and what loving response can you offer them?

_____

_____

_____

_____

_____

_____

_____

_____

_____

_____

_____

_____

What beliefs or ideas do you hold that create resistance to the concept of forgiveness? What is a healthier narrative you can replace it with?

Hoʻoponopono Practice

Hoʻoponopono is a long-held Hawaiian practice that helps with healing by bringing us to accept responsibility for the totality of our experience.

Hoʻoponopono, translated from the Hawaiian language, means "to correct, fix, and manage." This practice aims to help you open your heart to healing and love. When repeating and focusing intention on these phrases, you can unblock your consciousness and clear subconscious blocks that keep you from experiencing peace and happiness in your current situation, regardless of any past painful experiences. There is power in these words that will help you cultivate forgiveness, compassion, and love. Place both hands on your heart and repeat these phrases to your inner child several times.

- I'm sorry.

- Please forgive me.

- Thank you.

- I love you.

Nurturing Your Inner Child Every Day

L ike with all other inner work, inner child healing isn't something you do once or for a while and then are just done with. Instead, it's another powerful tool at your disposal that you can call upon whenever needed. More information, insight, and understanding are always surfacing waiting for us. Knowing how to confront what shows up with love and from a nonjudgmental perspective makes growth possible. As you learn to nurture your inner child through unconditional love, you extend this same energy to all aspects of yourself. From that space, self-care, radical self-acceptance, and self-compassion become a part of every move you make.

This section is all about helping you build upon the work you have already done, nurturing yourself by prioritizing your needs, and integrating this healing modality into your life through practices and exercises that weave perfectly into your daily routines. Healing isn't something you learn; it becomes a new standard for how you choose to live. It creates the foundation for joy and happiness, which is the true embodiment of a healed inner child.

Where do you struggle to show compassion toward yourself, and why do you think this is? What would it look like to be kinder to yourself in the future?

Where do you struggle to show compassion toward others, and why do you think this is? Do you see any connection between your ability to be compassionate toward yourself and others?

How does your wounded inner child project their pain or fear onto others? A good place to start here is to think about a current relationship where there is tension or strain.

How can you be more compassionate toward others, especially those who you may struggle to connect with? Each time you are compassionate toward others, you help heal your inner child.

The Thirty-Second Hug

The thirty-second hug is also known as the oxytocin hug because of the hormone released during extended periods of physical touch. The release of oxytocin eases anxiety and counteracts stress hormones. It also regulates the nervous system, promoting physical and emotional health.

Start by giving yourself thirty-second hugs periodically throughout the day. Aim for about three times a day: morning, afternoon, and evening. If you have a hard time remembering, try setting a reminder on your phone.

You can also induce the release of oxytocin by practicing extending long hugs to your partner, children, best friend, or family members.

Observing the Benefits of Self-Soothing

Use this page to document your experience with practicing the thirty-second hug.

Before the hug: Take a deep breath and notice how you feel before the thirty-second hug. In the first box below, note what you feel in your body or your energy. For example, do you feel tightness in your chest, anxious, heaviness somewhere in your body, and so on?

After the hug: Take another deep breath once you have finished and tune in to your body, mind, and spirit once again. Note the shift in the second box below.

HOW I FEEL BEFORE

HOW I FEEL AFTER

The more I extend love and compassion to myself, the more easily I can extend love and compassion to others.

An affirmation is a sentence that we can repeat to ourselves to uplift our thoughts and build our sense of self-worth, like the one on the previous page.

Use the space below to come up with your own positive affirmations. These could be phrases you wish you could have heard as a child or things you need to hear now. Write down as many as you can think of and then try saying them to yourself out loud.

Embody Self-Care

Proper self-care goes so far beyond spa days or hot baths. Don't get me wrong; those things are fantastic, so don't stop doing them! But when we learn to care for our needs on a moment-to-moment basis, we have genuinely mastered self-care.

What we need and desire today often reflects our past and what we didn't receive as a child. By tuning in to your needs with consistency and following the guidance given, you can effectively but indirectly reparent that wounded inner child.

Check in with yourself at least five times a day by pausing, taking a deep breath, and asking, "What do I need at this moment?" Trust the first thing that comes to mind, and don't second-guess yourself. Give yourself whatever you need at that moment. It may be movement, water, rest, laughter, touch, socialization, pleasure, or alone time, just to provide a few examples.

Each time I practice self-care, my inner child finds relief and comfort.

Self-Care Checklist

In this exercise, you get to explore different ways to care for yourself. In the following list, I have broken self-care into four main categories and included some fun ways to explore each. Try working your way through the list, placing a check next to the items you complete. Give yourself time in the coming weeks and months to work through as many items as you can.

Physical Self-Care

☐ Taking a walk outside

☐ Stretching or yoga

☐ Dancing

☐ Making a nutritious meal

☐ Doing some gardening

☐ Resting/napping

☐ Drinking more water

☐ Sitting in the sun

Emotional Self-Care

☐ Screaming, singing, making silly sounds, or doing anything vocal that releases emotional energy

☐ Crying

☐ Creating

☐ Asking for help

☐ Saying no to an extra commitment that isn't fulfilling

☐ Connecting with community

☐ Doing shadow work (see Resources on page 127 for more information)

☐ Keeping a gratitude journal

☐ Spending time with a pet

Mental Self-Care

- [ ] Reading a book
- [ ] Participating in a game night
- [ ] Learning a new hobby or trade
- [ ] Doing a short meditation
- [ ] Leaving work at work
- [ ] Taking a break from social media
- [ ] Practicing being mindful and intentional
- [ ] Listening to an inspiring speaker or an enriching podcast or watching an uplifting documentary
- [ ] Doing a puzzle

Social Self-Care

- [ ] Calling up an old friend or family member
- [ ] Inviting friends or family over for dinner
- [ ] Going out for Sunday brunch with someone
- [ ] Seeing a movie with a loved one
- [ ] Writing a letter to someone you love and sending it to them in the mail
- [ ] Planning a date night with a partner or good friend
- [ ] Attending a live music event

Connecting to Gratitude

There is something immensely healing that happens when we can connect to gratitude. While it takes time, eventually, we can even find reasons to be thankful for our past painful experiences and see how they shaped our lives for the better. This exercise will help connect you to this energy.

1. What positive aspects or experiences in your childhood are you thankful for?

....

....

....

....

2. What made these particular experiences enjoyable and special?

....

....

....

....

3. What is a painful aspect or experience in your childhood that you were able to eventually learn something from or that positively shaped you?

....

....

....

....

....

4. What family member, childhood friend, or allies are you thankful for, and why?

....

....

....

....

....

....

....

Make a Silly Sound

As adults, we can get caught up in the seriousness of day-to-day life. We juggle work, family, responsibilities, social obligations, and so on. As all this adds up, life can begin to feel heavy. To connect to your joyful inner child and elevate your mood, pause and make a silly sound. Do this a few times, and try not to be self-conscious. Remember, children are rarely concerned with how others are receiving them; they are too present in the moment to care. See how it feels to lean into your silly side among all the seriousness of life.

As we become adults, we tend to lose our sense of childlike wonder. Write about how you can bring more of this wonder into your life. It could be trying something unfamiliar, getting creative, exploring nature, or something else altogether.

The more grateful I feel,
the more joyful I am.

What have you learned from your inner child while completing this journal? What important lessons do you hope to carry forward?

Earlier in this journal you wrote a letter from your inner child to your adult self. Now it's time to flip the script and write a letter to your inner child from your current self. What words of comfort and support would you offer them? What would you like to tell them about their strength and resilience? What are you excited to share with them about your life now?

Take a moment to breathe in the accomplishment of completing this journal! What comes up for you emotionally? What are you proudest of?

A Final Note

Ultimately, inner child discovery and healing is a journey to deeper self-love and acceptance. It leads us gently to forgiveness of self and others, teaches us how to become better parents to ourselves, and inspires and empowers us to break generational wounds. As we extend love, compassion, acceptance, and forgiveness to ourselves and those who impacted us the most, we can better show up to the world and extend all of those beautiful things to others as well, making this world better than we found it.

Each time someone chooses healing over hurting, growth over stagnancy, and accountability over denial, they do an excellent service to the collective through the positive ripples they create. For choosing to do the hard work for the betterment of yourself and all, I send you my deepest gratitude. Don't underestimate the impact you have on this world. You deserve to be celebrated for your hard work, so invoke that inner child energy and get out and do something fun!

Resources

Books

Emotional Intelligence: Why It Can Matter More Than IQ
Based on new scientific research, this book by Daniel Goleman explores how the rational and the emotional mind work together to create our current perception and how these factors impact our experiences.

How to Do the Work: Recognize Your Patterns, Heal from Your Past, and Create Your Self
This book by Dr. Nicole LePera helps you recognize limiting belief patterns and confront conditioned thinking in order to reconnect with your true self.

It Didn't Start with You: How Inherited Family Trauma Shapes Who We Are and How to End the Cycle
This book by Mark Wolynn serves as an exploration of the connection between generational wounds and anxiety, depression, chronic pain, and other mental and physical disorders.

Judgment Detox: Release the Beliefs That Hold You Back from Living a Better Life
Written by Gabrielle Bernstein, this book gently guides you to understanding the deeper meaning and root cause of the judgments you hold so that you can release them and live a more joyful life.

Shadow Work Journal and Guide for Beginners

My shadow work journal and guide is full of advice and journal prompts to help you engage with the shadows and face the future with peace and confidence.

Taming Your Outer Child

This book by Susan Anderson offers a three-step program for overcoming self-sabotage and healing from abandonment.

Podcasts

High Vibe Podcast

On my show, *High Vibe Podcast*, my many guest speakers and I offer insight into matters of emotional well-being and personal growth with honesty and vulnerability.

SelfHealers SoundBoard

A podcast to help you recognize and confront your patterns, heal past painful experiences, and develop a deeper understanding of yourself. It is hosted by Dr. Nicole LePera and Jenna Weakland.

Spiritual Queen's Badass Podcast

Hosted by Emma Mumford, this podcast covers topics such as the law of attraction and spirituality to help you manifest the life you want.

References

Centers for Disease Control and Prevention. "Adverse
   Childhood Experiences (ACEs)." April 2, 2021.
   cdc.gov/violenceprevention/aces/index.html.

Sigal, John J., Vincenzo F. Dinicola, and Michael Buonvino.
   "Grandchildren of Survivors: Can Negative Effects of Pro-
   longed Exposure to Excessive Stress Be Observed Two
   Generations Later?" *Canadian Journal of Psychiatry* 33, no. 3
   (April 1988): 207–12. doi.org/10.1177/070674378803300309.

About the Author

 **Kelly Bramblett** is a trauma support coach and spiritual mentor who works with people from all over the world who are struggling with unresolved wounds. Kelly is a fully certified general life coach, trauma care specialist, law of attraction practitioner, emotional freedom technique practitioner, and Usui Reiki master teacher. Kelly's first book, *Alchemy of the Phoenix: From the Ashes of Trauma to the Light of Love*, continues to offer support for trauma survivors worldwide. She is also the author of the *Shadow Work Journal and Guide for Beginners*. You can learn more about Kelly's work by visiting her website at kellybramblett.com.

CPSIA information can be obtained
at www.ICGtesting.com
Printed in the USA
JSHW060031011122
32374JS00005B/25